Faith and Imagination

Keys to Effortless Living

Dr. Dara M. Lemite

Faith and Imagination: Keys to Effortless Living
Copyright © 2021 by Dr. Dara M. Lemite

All rights reserved. No part of this book may be reproduced or transmitted in any form or by any means without written permission from the author.

ISBN (978-0-578-94177-6)

Visit:
www.daramarieproductions.com

Available for speaking engagements, coaching, and live performances

Dedication

This book is dedicated to my son, Matthew. I pray that you will always walk by faith and use the gift of imagination to create the life you desire.

Table of Contents

Introduction 5

1: Know Who You Are 7

2: Speak to Your Mountain 23

3: Visualize It 39

4: Self- Talk......................................58

5: Eliminate Distractions................78

Introduction

Have you ever felt like there was more in store for you? That innate desire to have and want more out of life? Have you ever felt like you are not truly living out your life's purpose or just tired of the status quo? Something deep inside you is pushing for more, but you are not quite sure what that is. Something deep inside is telling you that you were created for more.

As believers, we were designed in the image of God. In the beginning, God created us to have dominion and authority over the situations in our lives. We were made to create. God wants us to live *flourishing and abundant lives* (John 10:10). To do so, we have to know and understand who we are and whose we are.

This book, Faith and Imagination, will give you strategies on how to create the life you were created to live by teaching you how to live by faith and utilize your imagination to create the life you deserve.

Chapter 1

Know Who You Are

"For we are His workmanship, created in Christ Jesus for good works, which God prepared beforehand that we should walk in them" (Ephesians 2:10 NKJV).

In the beginning, God made us in His image. As creations of God, we have the DNA of Him inside of us. We are children of the Heavenly Father. Therefore, we can be, do, or have anything in this life. It is so important to know who you are. When you know who you are, you are not moved, shaken, or dismayed by what occurs in the natural realm. We are spiritual beings who have a soul and live in a body. We are multi-dimensional. Then God said, *"Let us make mankind in our image, in our likeness, so that they may rule over the fish in the sea and the birds in the sky, over the livestock and all the wild animals, and over all the creatures that move along the ground.* Genesis 1:26 NIV)". God wants us to have dominion and authority over the situations in our lives. As believers, we should never feel helpless or live without solutions to the problems we face.

How do we learn and know who we are, you may ask? The answers are found in the word of God. We understand who we are by studying and reading His Word. As we apply the Word, we learn who God says we are. We know that we can do "*All things through Christ*" (Philippians 4:13). We then understand that we were created to overcome and outlast any challenge. We realize that there is a Greater One that lives inside of us. "*Greater is He, that is in me, than he that is in the world*"(1 John 4:4). We also learn that God's plan for our lives is great, and His plan is good (Jeremiah 29:11). As we study His Word, we see that God is faithful. He never gives up on us.

When you understand who you are in Christ, you will have a foundation to build your life. Your identity is not based on what you have or haven't done; however, it is solely based upon who God says you are. When we know who we are in Christ, we become a new creation. "*The old passes away, and all things become new*" (2 Corinthians 5:17). It is essential to know who you are in Christ because when you confidently know who you are in Him, you will move through life with boldness and clarity. Your identity in Him acts as a compass to guide your decisions and the way you live your life. The alignment in His purpose will be exact as Christ lovingly encourages you toward your divine destiny.

Not Knowing Who You Are

Now that I have covered what it takes to know who you are in Christ, I want to briefly share a story about not knowing your identity in Him. During high school, I was one of the top flutists. There were only four of them in my department, and I was one of them. I have always had a profound love of music. I remember hearing the flute as a child for the first time, and it gave me a feeling like no other! I knew right then, and there the flute was the instrument for me. I joined the band in fourth grade and continued to play throughout high school. I looked forward to attending college with such anticipation because I knew I was going to study `music. I was so excited to be following my passion and could not wait. Then it seems that somewhere along my musical journey, something shifted. When I was a freshman in college, I began to feel overwhelmed. I could not understand how something I loved so much suddenly caused me to feel so much anxiety. The apprehension and worry started to creep in as I attended rehearsals and classes. I began to compare myself to other musicians, and those feelings of not being good enough took over. Where was this coming from? My mind started to race and wander because I did not have a clue how this began. Before all of this, I felt confident in my musical talent and abilities. I believed I was more than capable, but I told myself I was not good enough when I arrived at Hofstra University's Music Department.

    As I look back, I know this was a lie from the pit of hell. You see, the enemy's job is to get you to abort your destiny. If he can fill your mind with doubt, fear, unbelief, and distractions, you will get off course. Our job as believers is to recognize when his forces are at work. The Bible says, *"For we wrestle not against flesh and blood, but against principalities, against powers, against the rulers of the darkness of this world, against spiritual wickedness in high places"*

(Ephesians 6:12)." And, since we know there are forces at work, we are to continue to "*walk by faith*" (2 Corinthians 5:7). When we walk by faith, we do not allow what we see in the natural to hinder what our spirit believes. When you walk by faith, you will be led by the truth located in God's Word rather than the deception found in the world.

Allow me to share another story about our purpose and identity in Christ. During Covid-19, I visited a nail salon, and the talk of vaccines was a very prevalent topic. At the time, there were only two of us in the establishment. I was sitting in one part of the salon allowing my manicure to dry, and the other lady was getting a massage in one of the massage chairs. I also did not know this woman, but I saw her before in the salon and discerned through interactions with others that she was not a friendly person. At that time, a woman walked into the salon but was not wearing a mask. I overheard her ask the salon owner if she should wear her mask, and he replied, "No, if you do not want to." The woman proceeded to walk over and sit down in a pedicure chair. I noticed this interaction, and I told myself that she would say something to that woman when this other woman gets out of the massage chair because she wasn't wearing a mask. As noted, when the woman in the massage chair got up, she noticed the woman in the pedicure chair was not wearing a mask and began "going off" about her not wearing a mask. The woman proclaimed how she is vaccinated and still wearing a mask. There was a brief exchange of words between the two before the woman screamed an expletive and walked out of the store. The woman sitting in the pedicure chair started crying and explained she had just lost her husband a few days ago. She said she came to the nail salon to get away and relax.

    I immediately went over to her and shared a few words of comfort, something I do pretty often as a chaplain. The ironic thing about this entire interaction was that I was right next to the woman who was not wearing a mask, yet I had no fear at all, unlike the other woman. I am always asking God for the message. Even amid chaos and madness, I knew a message was involved, so I asked the Lord to interpret the message for me as I left the nail salon. He then spoke to my spirit and reminded me that this happens when we do not know who and whose we are. As believers, we cannot trust in the things of man over the things of God. When you trust in the things of man, you will sway back and forth as a boat tossed upon the raging seas. You will not be on a solid foundation.

I am reminded of a famous hymn, "On Christ the solid rock I stand, all other ground is sinking sand." We must trust and hold on to the ever-present, non-changing hand of God. God knows everything about our lives. He knows exactly how to get us to our appointed destination. When you do not know who you are, every whim and utterance of society will move you. If you have not noticed, the world can be unstable at times. Our hope should be in God, who will never leave us or forsake us. He loves you with an everlasting love, (Jeremiah 31:3). Not knowing who you are will cost you. It will derail and abort your destiny; however, you will move forward into your God-given destiny when you know who you were created to be. You will not let hindrances stop you because that will push you towards all you were created to be.

Made to Create

Since we were created in the image of God, we can make the life we live, including how we experience it.

"*You are gods; you are all children of the Most High"* (Psalm 82:6 NLT). And, since we are created in His image, and He refers to us as little gods, we can create our reality. This means we have dominion and authority over the situations in our lives. *"You are fearfully and wonderfully made"* (Psalm 139:14). Once you genuinely know your identity and begin to accept it, you will start to walk in your God-given authority. You will not settle for less than you deserve. Life becomes limitless. We are not supposed to be overwhelmed by the situations of this world; we are to use our authority in Christ to shift our circumstances.

Created for Greatness

When we study His Word, we learn who we are and His promises for us. We recognize that we were created for greatness. We understand that we have dominion and authority and that we can overcome the challenges of this life. Since we are made in the image of God, we can create. When you realize that you are a co-creator with God, you will press into all that God has for you. The only limitations are the ones you manifest in your mind. "The first thing that we need to realize from the Scriptures is the power of

God's Word. We need to realize that this is a supernatural book. Like Moses' rod, it contains a power that isn't obvious when you first look at it. But, when you begin to understand it, its power actually is limitless." - Derek Prince

I would encourage you today to begin to study who God says you are. Once you start to learn who you are, you will move forward in what He calls you to do without hesitation. You will gain confidence because you know that the Greater One lives in you!

When you know who you are, you will no longer settle for a life that is less than. I am here to tell you every dream, every desire, every goal, every vision you can achieve. We have to walk by faith, know who we are, and press forward into everything God created us to be!

One day, while conversing with God, I asked Him about several things that I desire for my life. He spoke back to my heart and said, "*I created you to be here on earth to experience life to the best of your ability.* This is why the Word says, "*Beloved, I pray that you may prosper in all things and be in health, just as your soul prospers*" (3 John 1:2 NKJV).

We were never created to think or believe small. We were designed to create the life we desire. We were designed to be able to speak and think our life into existence. The Word says *to call those things that be not as though they are* (Romans 4:17). We are not supposed to look to the natural realm for confirmation or validation on the things we want. As believers, we are not supposed to be living and thinking from a limited standpoint because we serve a limitless God. There are no limits in Him! I honestly believe once you have the desire, that means you are supposed to have that what you've requested. For example, if you desire to write a book, you are supposed to write that book. Whatever God has placed inside of you, you are the person to fulfill that desire. Remember, you were destined for greatness. I believe God would not allow us to have dreams, goals, or desires that we could not fulfill. I do not believe God would give us life and then not have us accomplish our goals and dreams because that would be meaningless. As believers, we know God is powerful and mighty. And, since we are His children, why wouldn't He want us to be great too? You were created to create. God wants you to live an extraordinary life!

Self- Concept

To live the life that God has designed for us, we have to believe that we deserve it. Your core beliefs of who you are will manifest in your life. According to science, our subconscious mind is what dictates our thoughts, beliefs, and behaviors. We must have a healthy concept of self. For example, if you have deeply rooted feelings of unworthiness, you will experience things in your outer world to make you feel unworthy. It is vital to get our self-concept from the Word of God and who God says we are. Dr. Neil T. Anderson states, "The more you reaffirm who you are in Christ, the more your behavior will begin to reflect your true identity." I agree wholeheartedly.

Your foundational beliefs are what you create in your outer world. How you see yourself is how everyone else sees you. It is so important to have a healthy self-concept. Start describing yourself as the person you want to be. We need to believe at the core of our very being who God says we are, no matter what outside circumstances try to dictate. As believers, we can override circumstances when we step into the true essence of who we were created to be. You may want to know how do I change my self-concept? It is changed by using our thoughts and words. For example, if you do not feel worthy or loved, begin by speaking this affirmation; **I am confident and secure.** You can speak this out loud or begin to affirm it in your mind. God gave us the powerful gift to *"decree a thing"* (Job 22:28). Your self-concept is the ability to declare I am statements boldly. It matters who you genuinely think you are. This idea of self-concept is what creates your outer world. We have to change our old thoughts and persist in our new beliefs. We do this by consistently thinking and affirming who we are in every category of life. Until we change what we believe about ourselves within, nothing on the outside will change. We have to think about what God says we are at a core level.

You Have Authority

When God created us, He created us to have dominion and authority. This means that we have power over the situations in our lives. Your most extraordinary awareness is knowing who you are in Christ. When you know who you are in Christ, you will not be easily fooled or deceived by the deceptions of this world. *"For I am sure that neither death nor life, nor angels nor rulers, nor things present nor things to come, nor powers, nor height nor depth, nor anything else in all creation, will be able to separate us from the love of God in Christ Jesus our Lord"* (Romans 8:38- 39 ESV).

We are made with the characteristics of God. The Word says we are made in His image, and we can literally shift things around us. We should not feel overwhelmed, helpless, or have to succumb to life situations. We are indeed without limits if we would tap into that side of us. Using our spiritual authority allows us to transcend the limitations and troubles of life. *We have power over all the works of the enemy* (Luke 10:19). Use your authority!

Affirmations

- I am a child of God
- I was created to do great things
- I am blessed
- I can do all things through Christ
- I have incredible gifts and talents
- God has an excellent plan for my life
- I love myself
- I am victorious
- God chooses me
- I am worthy
- I am powerful
- I am loved
- I am a joint heir with Jesus
- I expect great things to happen in my life
- I have the peace of God
- I am God's workmanship
- I am complete in Christ
- I am an overcomer

Journal Questions

1. What steps will I take to begin to know who I am?

2. What affirmations will I speak daily?

Chapter 2

Speak to Your Mountain

"What you decide on will be done, and light will shine on your ways" (Job 22: 28 NIV).

"Truly I tell you, if anyone says to this mountain, 'Go, throw yourself into the sea,' and does not doubt in their heart but believes that what they say will happen, it will be done for them" (Mark 11:23 NIV). As believers, we have been given authority over the works of the enemy (Luke 10:19). This means that no matter what comes our way, we have the power to overcome it. We have to learn to speak to our mountains. In the scripture Mark 11:23, the mountain represents anything that is a challenge. When we begin to speak life over situations, things start to change. Our power is in the words we speak. The Word says that death and life is in the power of the tongue (Proverbs 18:21). Therefore, we have to learn to speak in alignment with God's Word. Always

choose to speak life. You will have victory over the situations in your life when you speak life.

Changing Circumstances

Several years ago, I went through a painful and heartbreaking divorce. Naturally, I experienced deep hurt and resentment. During this experience, my ex and I would have tumultuous arguments. At one point, things became really ugly, and I realized that all of this arguing wasn't worth it. There was someone more important than all of this, and he was my son. I realized I didn't want my son to see his parents arguing, using harsh words, and being unkind to each other. What kind of lasting impact would that have on his mind? I started to see the bigger picture and realized that I wanted my son to grow and be completely whole. Although his dad and I would no longer be together, I wanted Matthew to see us at peace, so I began to speak peace over the situation. I've heard from other people how divorce proceedings can take years, and things can drag out unnecessarily, which causes more pain, more hurt, more financial destruction, etc. I knew I wanted no part of that. So, every time my ex-husband would try to argue and be combative, I just kept telling him all I desire is peace. I believe I said it so much that I began to sound like a broken record. And that became a part of my strategy. Every time he would try to argue and start a fight, I would say all I want is peace. I remember telling him, " I don't want anything from you, all I want is peace."

When you are going through situations, all you can see is what is in front of you. As humans, we focus too much on the problem without realizing more is at stake. I began to realize that even though he and I would no longer be together, he would always be my son's father. That is one fact that I could not change. I realized it is better to be at peace than to live in strife. The Word says, "*Do all that you can to live in peace with everyone"* (Romans 12:18 NLT).

As believers, we forget at times that our power lies in the words we speak. "The tongue can bring death or life; those who love to talk will reap the consequences" (Proverbs 18:21 NLT). We have to realize we reap from the words we speak. Our words can genuinely bring life or death to a situation.

As I began to speak peace and life over that situation, things slowly began to change. It took some time. And, at times, honestly, I did not think we would have peace, but the peace we have now is truly a peace that surpasses human understanding (Philippians 4:7). Only God brings that kind of peace to the situation I once faced. It is *amazing*! From time to time, people ask me how did we get to that place? That place of peace, and I tell them we were not always peaceful. At one point, there was terrible strife; however, God laid it on my heart to begin to speak peace. I obeyed. I believe it was through my obedience to what God said that God moved on my behalf. Our once stressful relationship is now peaceful. I am genuinely thankful to God for that. My son now sees us at peace with one another. It is a beautiful thing. I want my son to realize although his parents are not together, we are still at peace with one another.

As believers, we have to realize that our choices have consequences that can affect the current and future generations. When you begin to take the focus off of you and place it on others, you see the situation more broadly. You begin to realize it is not all about you. I learned by speaking life to this situation that not only would I change the trajectory of my story, and I would also change my son's story. The impact of speaking life and speaking according to God's Word has incredible, lasting effects.

When you speak life, you begin to act like a thermostat and shift the very nature of everything around you. Like a thermostat changes the temperature in a room, you change everything around you by what you say. Things will have to adjust and change because our words have power. Words create, and you must remember this: *You will have what you say* (Mark 11:24).

Decree and Declare

In Job 22:28, it says, "*Thou shalt also decree a thing, and it shall be established unto thee: and the light shall shine upon thy ways.*" Whatever we decree and declare over our lives, it will be done. We have to trust that our words have power and that our words can shift the climate and atmosphere.

A while ago, I wanted to buy a folding bicycle. I wanted one that was portable and able to fold so it could be conveniently placed in the trunk of my car. I wanted one that folded because I did not want a bike rack on the top of my car. Those look so tacky and bulky to me, lol. It's just my preference, I guess. Second, I wanted to buy a bicycle second hand. I did not want to spend too much money on it since I was just getting back into cycling. Keep in mind; I had not been on a bike in twenty years! Well, I extended my search to Craigslist, where I found one for about $120. I thought to myself, wow, this bike must not be good. I even told my son Matthew about it. He told me, "Mom, like you, always tell me you will have what you say. If you think it's a bad bike, it will be. But, if you think it's a good bike, it will be". On my way to check out this bike, I kept telling myself, and even at one point said out loud, "It will be a good bike." Guess what? It turned out to be a great bike! The seller even allowed me to ride it up and down the block a couple of times. The bike was just as I said it would be. It was perfect. This was especially good for someone like me who was just getting back into bike riding. I received what I said. I was so thankful! God not only honors our faith, but He honors the words we speak in faith.

Walk by Faith

The Word says we are to walk by faith and not by sight (2 Corinthians 5:7). When we walk by faith, we allow God to move in our lives, and the miraculous happens. Pastor Christine Caine once said, "Build your life on the truth of the Word of God and not the facts of your circumstances." Please understand your past does not define your future and what God wants to do through you. Your circumstances can change. It is up to you to believe, speak, and walk by faith. In my life, I found that every time I chose to walk by faith and not by sight, God moved on my behalf. When we walk by faith, we trust God and what He says in His Word. We take Him at His Word and act upon it. *Faith without works is dead* (James 2:17).

As I speak on faith, I am reminded of a story I'd like to share about a friend who told me about her friend who believed God for something big in her life. The lady was an attorney but no longer wanted to be one because her heart's desire was to become a judge. She told several people about what she wanted, and they told her about the obstacles she would possibly face and how it would take a long time to accomplish such a huge goal. The people she confided in made it seem it would take years to happen. With exemplary faith, this young lady desired the best not only for herself but for her autistic daughter, who lights up her life! Long story short, something that would have taken years to accomplish happened in a matter of months! There were all these tremendous obstacles in the natural, but she walked by faith and overlooked the challenges. She kept believing in faith no matter what it looked like. Sometimes, the human side of us may want to justify to others because we believe in faith. I know because I used to do that. If a person did not believe, I felt I would have to convince them. I would do the going back and forth thing. Not nastily or forcefully, but I just felt compelled to convince them to walk by faith and trust the Lord.

The older I get, the more I realize that faith is truly trusting God, walking with Him, and allowing Him to guide you in various areas in your life. Faith is a calm assurance that what we believe and know is true. *Faith comes by hearing and hearing by the Word of God* (Romans 10:17). When we walk by faith, God will honor our faith.

At present, I no longer feel that I have to convince someone to believe. I just plant the seed and allow God to water it to make it grow (1Corinthians 3:7). I believe as we walk by faith, it will encourage others to walk by faith too. We need to demonstrate our faith by living our lives and believing in the truth of God's Word.

We are not supposed to be hindered by what shows up in the natural. We are to walk by faith and speak according to God's Word.

Commanding Your Morning

As believers, we have the authority to speak our day into existence. Often, you hear people say, "I hope today will be a good day." When, in fact, we can speak to our day for it to be a good day just by the words we speak. Every day, I declare, today will be a good day because I said so, in Jesus' name. We can command our morning. Just as we drive our cars and use the steering wheel to direct us, we can lead our days and our lives by the words we speak. Use your words to "steer" your life in the direction you want to go. Try to discipline yourself to only speak about things that you want to experience. Speak words of wealth, healing, abundance, prosperity, wellness, etc. Watch God move as you speak in faith. To the finite mind, speaking your day into existence may seem foolish, but this is how we were truly designed. Our Creator created us to be able to speak the things we want into existence. "*Instead, God chose things the world considers foolish to shame those who think they are wise. And He chose things that are powerless to shame those who are powerful*" (1 Corinthians 1:27 NLT).

Often, when we think about decreeing and declaring, we think about using it for big things, tremendous things, life-altering things. I genuinely believe we are to use our faith and imagination daily. It should not just be for use in crisis.

Seasoned with Salt

Let your conversation be gracious and attractive so that you will have the right response for everyone (Colossians 4:6 NLT). We know salt is a seasoning. Salt not only gives food its flavor, but it makes food taste better. We also know that too much salt is not good either. There has to be balance. I believe this is why the Bible tells us that our conversations should be seasoned with salt. We have to know what to say, when we should say it and how to say it. Our words not only impact us, but they also impact others. This is why we need to choose our words carefully because words have power. They create. The very things you speak on can and will show up in your outer world.

Since our words have power, we must constantly engage our conversations towards the things we want. Speak only about what you want. Try at best not to speak anything negative. I know that can be a challenge at times because we are still human. Life is a daily battle, and we still face challenges and things that can be disheartening. As believers, we should try to focus and speak on inspiring and uplifting conversations. *"For by your words you will be justified, and by your words, you will be condemned"* (Matthew 12:37 NKJV). We have to speak life. To get through life and live successfully, we must choose to speak life.

Words have creative power. The words that we speak affect how we feel. Make it a habit of being aware of the words that come from your mouth. Speak about things that you want to see show up in your life. Stop speaking doubt, fear, unbelief, or anything negative. As believers, we are to "*Call those things that be not as though they are*" (Romans 4:17).

Angels on Assignment

Did you know when we speak according to God's Word, it puts angels to work? When we speak life and choose to speak to our mountains, it allows angels to work on our behalf. The Word says, "*Angels hearken unto the Word of the Lord.*"(Psalm 103:20).

Several years ago, I experienced a bad car accident that totaled my car. I recall driving down the road when a car ran the stop sign. I tried to swerve my car to avoid being hit; however, my vehicle was directly impacted. My car spun out of control before stopping on a lawn. I remember being extremely afraid at the time. I called out to God to help me and protect me as my car spun out of control. I truly believe that day God assigned His angels to cover me. Although my car was gone, I lived to tell the story.

I thank God for His hand of protection. As believers, when we call on God and speak His Word, He will move on our behalf.

It is so important to speak life over yourself. As believers, we need to stop talking about our problems and begin to speak solutions. Choose daily to speak to your mountains. When you speak to your mountains, they will move!

Affirmations

- I choose to speak life daily
- I speak in alignment with God's will for my life
- My words have power
- My words create
- I believe in myself
- I speak faith-filled, encouraging words
- I am blessed
- I am grateful
- I have everything I need and want
- I walk in abundance
- My life is flourishing
- I can do what I put my mind to
- I move forward daily in expectation
- I am an ambassador of Christ
- I have direct access to God
- I trust God's plan for my life
- My life is beautiful
- My life elevates daily
- I believe who God says I am

Journal Questions

1. What area(s) of my life do I need to speak to?

2. What affirmations will I use to speak to that situation?

_____
_____
_____
_____
_____
_____
_____
_____
_____
_____
_____
_____
_____
_____
_____
_____
_____
_____

Chapter 3

Visualize It

"Where there is no vision, the people perish: but he that keepeth the law, happy is he" (Proverbs 29:18).

It is vital to have a vision if you want to know where you're going. This is why the Word says, *"Write the vision; make it plain on tablets, so he may run who reads it"* (Habakkuk 2:2 ESV). When there is a vision for your life, you know where you're going and, you know what you want to accomplish—having a vision weeds out things that are unnecessary to where you are headed. A vision will streamline the things you need to do and the things you need to accomplish. Having a vision helps you to eliminate things that may be a hindrance to achieving your vision.

Thoughts proceed vision. In order to have a vision, you must think about what you want. Once you think about what you want, you can create a clear picture in your mind. This is what we call visualizing. Just like our words create, so does our thoughts. *"For as he thinks in his heart, so is he"* (Proverbs 23:7 NKJV).

I believe if we want to visualize correctly, we need to use our imagination. Our imagination has the potential to create amazing ideas! Remember when we were children, we dreamed of vast visions and ideas. We played make-believe as we went about becoming our favorite invincible superheroes without any hindrances or limitations. Yet, when we become older, that imaginative part of our brain somehow gets cut off. Albert Einstein once said, "Imagination is everything. It is the preview of life's coming attractions". Our imagination is necessary to see past the limitations of the natural realm we live. When you focus only on what you know, you will notice lack, limitations, and things that do not seem possible, but when you tap into your imagination, you open your mind to a world of possibilities. Imagination creates reality. This is why the Bible says, *"As a man thinks in his heart, so is he"* (Proverbs 23:7). Whatever we think, we become. Our thoughts are more powerful than people realize. Our imagination is like the movie screen of our mind. God gave us an imagination so that we can create the life we desire. Our imagination is a tool given to us by God. God *wants us to live our best life* (3 John 2). If you can see it in your mind, it is only a matter of time before it shows up in your outer world.

God gives us clear instructions on what we are to think. *"Finally, brethren, whatsoever things are true, whatsoever things are honest, whatsoever things are just, whatsoever things are pure, whatsoever things are lovely, whatsoever things are of good report; if there be any virtue, and if there be any praise, think on these things"* (Philippians 4:8). God wants us to focus our thoughts on inspirational and uplifting things. How do you do that if your outer world is showing something different? You go there in your imagination.

Many Thoughts

According to science, on average, we think anywhere between 60,000- 70,000 thoughts a day. That's a lot of thinking! Wouldn't it be in our best interest to think thoughts in alignment with what we want? I believe that our lives follow our thoughts. In order to see the manifestation of the things we desire, we have to think in the direction of the things we want to achieve. Once we begin to understand that our thoughts create, we will choose to think differently. I believe things happen in the spiritual realm first before it manifests naturally as there is a delay in this realm. Since we are created in the image of God, we are to think as God would want us to believe. In the beginning, God thought it, God spoke it, and then He saw what He said. We are to create in the same manner as God did.

We must get on top of our thoughts and manage our thoughts on purpose. Think on purpose. Do not entertain every idea just because it shows up in your mind. Make sure your thoughts are to your benefit. If you do not want it to show up in your reality, try not to think about it. For example, if you believe in wealth and financial freedom, think of abundance, wealth, prosperity, etc. Focus your thoughts on having a surplus of money and the things you would do with that. Think about the ways you would bless others with an abundance of finances.

The Power of Vision

Having a vision helps keep you anchored due to life's ups and downs. "*I have told you these things, so that in me you may have peace. In this world you will have trouble. But take heart! I have overcome the world"* (John 16:33 NIV).

The way we view these challenges is how we will get through them. Vision helps keep your focus forward. When you have a vision for your life, you are no longer looking backward but now looking ahead. People who have a vision tend to have strong faith and hope for the future. They realize that what is ahead is better than what has been. They know and trust God to do "*exceedingly and abundantly"* (Ephesians 3:20) in their lives. People with vision tend to be optimistic. They look at the bright side of things, the possibilities.

Your Thoughts Create

I knew a woman who also experienced a bad car accident. Although she survived and her car had significant damage, she revealed that she never fully recovered. The accident caused her to be filled with anxiety and fear as she spoke about bad drivers on the road. Do you know what else happened? She was involved in several more car accidents. I believe this was due to her fearful thoughts. Once again, our thoughts create because we were created to create. We must learn to choose our thoughts and words wisely. Our words will reap a harvest. Whatever we think, be it good or bad, we will experience in our reality. *"For as he thinketh in his heart, so is he"* (Proverbs 23:7).

Completely Whole

Several years ago, when my son was in second grade, he was diagnosed repeatedly with Strep throat. I would take him to the doctor, and she would prescribe the appropriate medicine to rid him of this ailment. I administered the meds, and in a few days, he would recover, but it would come right back. I shared this with a coworker, and she said, "Usually when it keeps coming back, the doctor may suggest his tonsils be removed." Well, that was all I needed to hear. As soon as she mentioned that, a bit of fear started to creep in. Little did she know, I had some of those thoughts of my own. At the time, I wondered if this disease keeps coming back, he may have to have them taken out, which I did not want. I did not want my little boy to undergo surgery. At the time, I did not realize what I was doing. I kept imagining Matthew as completely healed from Strep. Every time I would think of him getting strep, I would flip the thoughts to positive ones. I visualized him being healthy and whole. It has been several years since Matthew has had strep throat. It completely vanished! I truly believe by visualizing and seeing him completely healed; it was already done. What we see in our mind we will experience in our outer world. The key is to see it done, see it finished.

See It Within

If we want to see something without, we must see it within. Our thoughts are so powerful that the mental images we create in our minds will be seen in our reality. The unseen realm is the spiritual realm. The seen realm is the natural realm. What we see with our human eyes is subject to change if we believe it. *"So we fix our eyes not on what is seen, but on what is unseen since what is seen is temporary, but what is unseen is eternal"* (2 Corinthians 4:18 NIV*).* Our job as believers is to stand firm in the unseen, realizing that everything we see is subject to change. That is what the Word says. If you can see it within your imagination, it is only a matter of time that you will see it become a reality. The great thing about seeing things within is that there are no limits. Our imagination is vast. It is truly a gift that God gives us so that we can create continually.

Your Powerful Imagination

To see a thing, we have to see it in our minds first. How do you do that? You see through your imagination. Your imagination is a gift that God has given you to create the life you desire and deserve. We have to choose to use our imagination actively and intentionally. *God wants you to enjoy life and live abundantly."* (3 John 2 NKJV)". Our imagination is something we should use daily and often. This is where we can visualize and create the life we desire. A famous author, Neville Goddard, once said,

"Imagination and faith are the secrets of creation." When we use our faith and move in imagination, we create the things we desire. Please understand, faith is a higher realm. Faith is above the lack and limitations of this life. When you use your imagination, you can visualize past what you see in the natural. Right now, I would like you to think about something you believe God for. Take a few seconds, close your eyes and visualize. See that specific desire in your mind's eye. Now, open your eyes. How do you feel? If done correctly, you may think that what you envisioned is real because it's your imagination at work. Remember the story I told you about the bicycle I purchased on Craigslist? Before I received the bike, I spoke well about the bike, but I also imagined that the bike would be a good one. I visualized it in my mind before I even looked at the bike.

Years after going through a painful divorce, I knew I wanted to relocate to another town. I thought it would be best to move closer to my parents, and I desired to be only about 10 minutes away. I knew I wanted my son to be a part of a good school district to excel in school and learn a lot. As I reflect on where I live, I realize I imagined my place of residence. Before living in this town, I imagined living in a quiet area with an open layout. I desired something spacious and having wood floors throughout my home. During the home showing with the realtor, I thought about how much I liked the place. Yes, this was the one! This is what I envisioned. It checked off everything I had included in my mind or my mental checklist. Fast forward to today, and I still live in this quiet town. The place is beautiful, and my son and I are happy to be here.

Your imagination is such a powerful tool if you would use it. I encourage you today to use the tool of imagination. It was given to you by God to create the life you want to live. People say life is not perfect, but I believe it can be by the thoughts we think and using our imagination to create. Nothing exists unless it is imagined first. Everything begins with imagination, just as God created the world with His imagination.

Everything you see in the natural realm was first seen in the mind of someone. For example, the car you drive, the house you live in, the clothes you wear, etc., were first seen in someone's mind. I can only imagine when Henry Ford thought about when he made the first car. People probably thought he was crazy and didn't know what he was talking about! Before cars, the mode of transportation was horse and buggy or using our two feet.

Candace Thoth once said, "Imagination will get you anywhere in rapid speed, in ways that the logical mind could never construct." The physical world is our thoughts, or our imagination pushed out. If we want to change what is showing up in our outer world, we must change what we are picturing in our minds. What are you imagining? Use your imagination to create the life you desire. I believe we are here to create the life we want because God would not allow us to have different hopes, dreams, and visions and not allow them to come to pass. That we would desire such things, not fulfill them, and then die. What kind of life would that be? His Word says that we are to live life abundantly (John 10:10). Your imagination will take you beyond the limitations of this natural realm. Not only were we created to speak things into existence, but we can think them into existence too. That is so powerful! We are more powerful than we think. "*I can do all things through Christ who strengthens me*" (Philippians 4:13 NKJV). As believers, we can do all things through God's power. When we allow God's super to get on our natural, there is nothing we cannot do! God created us so that we can create what we want when we want. Use your faith and imagination and think about the things you want to create in your life. Shut out the 3D realm, go dream, persist in your desire because that is when what you want will show up. Keep in mind that anytime you are checking the 3D realm, the natural realm, for confirmation, you are saying that you do not trust your God-given power to create. This is the power that God gave you. His Word says, "*Greater works we will do*" (John 14:12). We are powerful, creative beings. We are to create through the use of our faith and our imagination.

When we visualize, we see past our current state. Visualization allows us to see the possibilities for our lives. Visualization allows us to go deeper spiritually, and in turn, we will see the manifestation of the things we visualize.

At the present moment, there is something that I have been praying and believing God for. Every day without fail, I see the picture of what I am thinking and desiring. At times, I close my eyes and visualize it. I can see it clearly in my mind. I see the details vividly. It's so real at times that when I open my eyes, I am shocked that it is not here yet, but I know it's on the way. Every day I see it in my outer world.

I encourage you to speak life and visualize the direction of your life. When you imagine, you are focusing on the desired results. If you can see it in your mind, it is only a matter of time to experience it in your outer world. Our imagination helps us to create the life we desire. Our vision was given to us by God. The Word says, "*You will make your way prosperous, and then you will have good success*" (Joshua 1:8). Always speak words, focus, and stay in alignment with what God says you can have and do!

Affirmations

- I visualize my goals
- I see God's favor on my life daily
- I envision living the life of my dreams
- I visualize living a life of happiness
- If I see it in my mind, I will see it in my outer world
- I visualize everything working out for me
- My mind is clear and focused
- I see myself as prosperous
- Greater is coming
- My thoughts are powerful and create
- I see myself living a fulfilled life
- I have a renewed mind
- I am the head and not the tail
- Wealth is my portion
- I am valued
- I am successful
- I am chosen to bear fruit
- I have direct access to God
- God anoints me
- I am abundant

Journal Questions

1. In what ways will I use visualization to enhance my life?

_____
_____
_____
_____
_____
_____
_____
_____
_____
_____
_____
_____
_____
_____
_____
_____
_____

2. What affirmations will I speak to help me visualize?

Chapter 4
Self- Talk

"Death and life are in the power of the tongue, And those who love it will eat its fruit" (Proverbs 18:21 NKJV).

During the summer of 2016, I began experiencing some discomfort in my chest. I remember sitting in the nail salon waiting for my nails to dry, and suddenly I began to feel nauseous. I decided I would go home, take a shower and take a nap. When I laid down, I didn't feel better and decided to go to the urgent care down the street. When I walked in, I explained to them what I was experiencing. Immediately, the doctor took me into the room and took my vitals. He tried not to look concerned, but he informed me that he wanted me to go to the hospital by ambulance. At that point, I started to feel worried. I was thinking to myself, what is happening to me? Before going into the ambulance, I called my parents to inform them of what was happening. Fast forward to the emergency room, and the doctor proceeds to tell me they believe there was a clot in my lung. I remember seeing the concern and sadness on my Dad's face. That broke me inside. My mom, a retired registered nurse, tried to hide her worries so that I wouldn't worry, but I know she was concerned too.

I remember saying to myself, God, it's you and me. In the Bible, the prophet Hezekiah received word that he was about to die (2 Kings 20). There's a point in the story where Hezekiah turns his face to the wall. In that emergency room, my bed was against the wall. I remember turning to face the wall, and as Hezekiah did, I began to talk to God and spoke healing affirmations over my life. That was my self-talk time. At that moment, I spoke every promise from God's Word that I remembered. I began to speak life in my mind. No matter what the doctor was saying, I chose to believe God's Word over her word. I remember the doctor informing me of the various tests that they would have to perform on me. She also told me they would do a CT scan. I remember them taking so many vials of blood. I believe they poked and prodded me for everything known to man, lol.

The following day, two female doctors walked into my room, smiling and very pleasant. They informed me that after extensive testing, they could not find anything wrong. All of this transpired in less than 24 hours. I know it was due to my inner talk. Throughout the evening, I continued to speak affirmations over my life. I kept saying in my mind; I shall live and not die to declare the works of the Lord (Psalm 118:17). There is such power when we come into an agreement. The Word speaks of how can two walk together unless they agree. As believers, we must be particular about the things we come into agreement with. *Death and life are in the power of the tongue* (Proverbs 18:21).

You can create your reality through your self-talk. Self-talk is the conversations you have with yourself. What are you saying to yourself throughout the day? Remember, we think all day. As I mentioned earlier, according to science, we think on average of 60,000-70,000 thoughts per day. That is a lot of thinking and a lot of ideas that need to be filtered. Please understand, your thoughts are personal to you. One person can be thinking thoughts of wealth, while another person is thinking thoughts of lack. Both will manifest and show up in their world because thoughts create. Since we know that words have power, and our thoughts create, it is in our best interest to focus on the best inner speech possible. The way to command your subconscious mind is through your thoughts. We must stay focused and disciplined on the things we want to create in our lives. Your self-talk and your inner thoughts are how you view yourself and everything around you. Your thoughts create. The quality of life you experience is related to the quality of your thoughts. You are constantly creating your life whether you know it or not.

The things we speak on and think about all day long will eventually show up. These things will become a part of our experience. When God created us, He created us in His image. He also gave us the gift of free will. We can choose how we will experience life. *"Today, I have given you the choice between life and death, between blessings and curses. Now I call on heaven and earth to witness the choice you make. Oh, that you would choose life, so that you and your descendants might live!"* (Deuteronomy 30:19 NLT).

Mental Diet

We have the power to create the life we want through our inner dialogue. Our internal conversations are like affirmations we speak over ourselves. Neville Goddard said, "Everything in the world bears witness of the use or misuse of man's inner talking." Your self-talk is like a mental diet. When you are on a diet, you discipline yourself in terms of what you eat. You become particular about what you put into your body. Likewise, when you are on a mental diet, you discipline yourself in terms of what you think and become particular about the things you take into your mind. When you are on a physical diet, your body begins to change and conform to what you consume. On a mental diet, your mind, thoughts, emotions, and actions start to fit and adjust to what you are feeding your mind. Due to this shift in the mind, your outer world will begin to conform to match what you believe to be true. "How do you keep a strict mental diet? You watch your thoughts throughout the day. Are the majority of my thoughts right now going with or towards my desire or against my desire? Am I thinking from lack right now? Constantly check in with yourself. That is what a strict mental diet is. "If you don't, you go back to your old programming and thoughts that do not serve you."-Ani

Inner Conversations

How are you speaking to yourself? What are you talking about? Your inner dialogue consists of the conversations you have with yourself. They are your innermost thoughts. Whether we acknowledge it or not, we think all day long, and our thoughts sometimes can't be shut off. It is in our best interest to think thoughts that serve us and speak kindly to ourselves. Whatever we believe consistently becomes true. Thoughts become things. Our inner conversations will become a reality. In the past, a person who spoke to themselves was considered crazy; however, now we know that our thoughts create what we understand about the subconscious mind. To change our reality, we must change our inner conversations. If you do not want to experience something in your reality, you must turn your attention away from it.

Too often, we are putting our attention on the wrong things. We focus on the negative things that do not serve us. At times, we do not realize that our focus on something, whether positive or negative, is what holds it in place. Your awareness of a thing is what keeps it there. "So what are you saying at every moment? Watch it! Be careful of what you are saying because your whole vast world is this inner conversation pushed out."- Neville Goddard

Your inner world affects your outer world. It has always been that way. From the beginning, when God created the world, He thought and spoke it into existence. We make our world and what we experience in life through our thoughts- inner conversations. Begin to have conversations in your mind about things that are of your highest good. Think about things that you are believing Him for. *"If you believe, you will receive whatever you ask for in prayer"* (Matthew 21:22 NIV). Your inner speech is what manifests. Everything starts from within. Whatever we dwell on is what creates. Dwell on things as if they are already confirmed, and then they will show up in your reality. Your inner conversations are those thoughts that are looping through your mind. These are the thoughts that persist in your mind all day long. We must learn how to create a new story. Persist with that story in our minds, and eventually, it will show up. The thoughts we constantly persist in create the manifestations. Joseph Murphy said, "All of us have our own inner fears, beliefs, opinions. These inner assumptions rule and govern our lives. A suggestion has no power in and of itself. Its power arises from the fact that you accept it mentally." When you want to experience something different, shift your inner dialogue. Quitting is not an option! We persist in our new thoughts, affirmations, and beliefs until it shows up. Once it shows up, it becomes a part of your experience. Your assumptions lead you to believe that it will always be that way. We have to think to the point of acceptance. "If I, in my imagination, could go right in and possess it and clothe myself with the feeling of the wish fulfilled, actually clothe myself with it by assuming that it's done now until I feel natural in that assumption and that assumption though at the moment denied by my senses, if persisted in will harden into fact."- Neville Goddard.

Anytime we feel down or discouraged, I believe it's because we focus too much on the natural realm, this 3D dimension. Joseph Murphy said, "Cease believing in the false beliefs, opinions, superstitions and fears of humankind. Begin to believe in the eternal verities and truths of life, which never change. Then, you will move onward, upward, and Godward." According to the Word of God, we are spirit, soul, and body. We have to remember we are spiritual beings that live in a body. We have to operate out of our spirit more than in the fleshly realm. When we focus too much on what we pick up with our natural eyes, it can cause discouragement. I always say you do not allow what you see with your natural eyes to hinder what your spirit believes. Anytime I am not feeling my best self, I start to think deeper, and I realize it because I am focusing too much on what is showing up in my outer world rather than focusing on what I am creating in my inner world, as within so it is without. *We walk by faith and not by sight* (2 Corinthians 5:7).

Life is a mirror. It reflects within from the person who you think and believe yourself to be. Everything in your life is going to reflect what dominantly you think is true. Therefore, staying on top of our inner conversations is essential. When you shift in your mind, your outer world will shift too. The life you experience aligns with the thoughts you think. Neville

Goddard said, "Everything in the world bears witness of the use or misuse of man's inner talking."

I love walking and living by faith because you do not need anyone's approval. No one can see your innermost thoughts. You can believe and speak in your mind whatever you want about yourself. For example, if you believe you are a millionaire, your inner conversations need to be about wealth. Start to think thoughts of wealth. Begin to speak affirmations in your mind about wealth. See yourself now as a millionaire. Your outer will start to reflect your inner world. Neville Goddard once said, "An assumption, though false, if persisted in, will harden into fact." Whatever internal conversations we have consistently will eventually become a reality in our 3D world.

This is what is meant by assumptions hardening into facts. To change the world around us, how we live life, and what we experience, we must change our inner conversations to match what we want to experience. As long as you are alive, this power to create is yours. Begin to use your God-given authority. Speak and think about what you want. Let your inner conversations match your desires. What you want, wants you. It is already waiting for you.

Peace Beyond Human Understanding

As I previously shared, my divorce was extremely painful. The separation process at times was not peaceful. We argued at times and were unkind to one another. At the time, this situation brought out a side that I did not know was there. Going through situations like that can bring you out of character, if you know what I mean. At one point through all of this, I just wanted peace. I realized that our son was young, and we would have to be in each other's lives, whether I liked it or not. I began to see the bigger picture. I wanted Matthew to grow up whole and happy and not experience the harmful effects of a painful divorce with two parents who were constantly at odds with one another. For this to happen, there had to be a shift in my mind. Amidst all of the chaos, I began to speak peace in my mind. Even when my ex-husband would try to argue, I just started to say to him, "I want peace."

To be honest, that was all I wanted. In my mind, there were only two options. Either we would deal with each other in chaos and have to be in court constantly, or we would deal with each other in peace, which would be better for us, and more importantly, our son, Matthew. I started to envision in my mind co-parenting Matthew and being cordial with one another. Anytime the situation would come to my mind, I would speak peace over it. I would also affirm peace over the situation. The Word says, "*You will have what you say*" (Mark 11:24).

Shift Your World

When you shift your words and inner conversations, the world around you will move to match what you have said. Neville Goddard said, "Most people are unaware of the fact that our inner conversations are the causes of the circumstances of our life."

Whatever you want in life, just decide on it. You do not need confirmation from the outer world. Everything starts with you. If you can see it in your mind, you will see it in your external world. It will become a part of your life experience. Many people do not realize the power and authority that God gave us (Genesis 1:26). Transformation happens when we shift to God's way of thinking (Romans 12:2). Old ways won't open new doors. Doing things the same way will not produce a different result. We have to shift our perspective and elevate our thinking. To be fully awakened in a sleeping world is a level of elevation that some people will never realize.

Remove Old Programming

At times when we are moving forward in life, old programming creeps up. Old programming consists of old thoughts that no longer serve you. We have to remember who we are. We are created in the image of God because his DNA is inside of us. Part of the problem is the programming that we received in the past is still a part of us. We have to let go of past programming to push forward into everything God created us to be. The old programming will try to hold you back to not move forward into what God has for you. For example, if a person has struggled in the past financially. Old programming will have them believe that they will always not have money and always struggle. One belief may be that they do not have opportunities to make money and move into abundance. Another example may be a person who has experienced bad relationships. Old programming will have someone believe that they will never have a good relationship. They may believe that all men or women cheat because those people do not know how to be faithful. These thoughts or programming are of no use to anyone. They do not serve you nor help you elevate to the next level. To push forward, we have to let go of old programming. *"Don't copy the behavior and customs of this world, but let God transform you into a new person by changing the way you think. Then you will learn to know God's will for you, which is good, pleasing, and perfect"* (Romans 12:2 NLT).

Speak Life

"You will also declare a thing, And it will be established for you; So light will shine on your ways" (Job 22:28 NKJV). There is such power in the words we speak. As people, we have been conditioned to believe that we want things that we cannot have. You may see a nice car or a lovely home and think you cannot have it. When the truth is the fact that you desire it, you are supposed to have it. I believe God gives us downloads that are clues to what we were created for, our purpose on this earth. If we want to

see it, we have to move in faith and speak in confidence.

As believers, we have the power to speak things into existence. We should always choose to speak life, speak in faith, and believe God to move on our behalf. Too often, people talk about the opposite, which is fear. We should never allow the natural realm to hinder what our spirit believes. Fear is false evidence appearing real. When you do not know what to say, speak life. When words seem to fail you, speak life. God does not renege on His Word. Zig Ziglar said, "Fear is faith in reverse." Let your faith override your fear. Fear moves the hand of God and causes miracles, signs, and wonders to flow into your life.

Forgetting the Past

I recall once having a conversation with someone who expressed that in order to move forward into what God has for you, you must deal with your past by diving into past hurts and reflecting on them. I disagree with this. I believe too much reflecting on the past is what causes people to remain stuck. If you are looking at your past, how can you see your future? When God wants to do a new thing in your life, you must look ahead. As believers, we should look at things as information and ask the Lord for revelation. Focusing too much on the past will keep you from moving into all that God has created you to be. You can look at the past to reflect on what needs to be changed and how it helped you grow into becoming who you are. During a harrowing season in my life, my Bible teacher said to me, "The breaking of you is the making of you." At that time, I did not realize what she meant. But now I do. Pain is what pushes us to our purpose. Had we not experienced any pain, we would not learn our strengths. That season of my life not only prepared me for 2020 but it reminded me of how faithful God is to us. When so many people around me were bugging out, I was able to stay grounded in my faith. I believe God brought me through other things in my life, and I fully trusted Him to carry me through. He did just what he would say he would do.

As believers, we should try at best not to hold on to our past. Use it as steppingstones into your future. We have to stop being stuck and not allow our past to define our future. There is more ahead of you than behind you when you know that God has great things in store for you. *"Brothers and sisters, I do not consider myself yet to have taken hold of it. But one thing I do: Forgetting what is behind and straining toward what is ahead"* (Philippians 3:13 NIV).

Affirmations

- I am amazing
- I love myself
- Life is effortless for me
- Everything works out for me
- I always have the best of everything
- Life is easy for me
- My thoughts are powerful
- I am the best version of me
- I am confident in myself
- I am blessed with many gifts and talents
- Life is beautiful
- Success is my birthright
- Prosperity is my birthright
- I have everything I need and want in abundance
- I am walking in divine favor
- I am flowing in my gifts
- I am brilliant
- My gifts make room for me
- I am walking by faith
- I am flowing in my purpose
- God's favor goes before me

Journal Questions

1. In what ways will I use self-talk to enhance my life?

2. What self-talk affirmations will I use daily?

Chapter 5

Eliminate Distractions

"If you are faithful in little things, you will be faithful in large ones. But if you are dishonest in little things, you won't be honest with greater responsibilities" (Luke 16:10 NLT).

I remember once being called to a specific assignment. In other people's eyes, it may have seemed like a downgrade and something that was beneath me. Someone even said to me, "Gosh! Why are you doing that? Such a waste of talent!" When you know who you are in Christ, you know that things do not just happen. If you trust God, nothing is just a coincidence. Things are done on purpose. Your steps are ordered by God. He will put us in unusual places in unusual positions at times. To the finite believer, it may look foolish or unsubstantial but trust God. He knows exactly what He is doing and what He wants to do through you.

While in this assignment, I knew that the Lord sent me there for a specific purpose. When we go through things, it is never about us. We are just the vessel He is using to get His purpose fulfilled on the earth. This is why the Word says, *"The Lord will fulfill His purpose for me"* (Psalm 138:8 ESV). God sees every area of our lives and knows precisely how to get us to our appointed destination. *"Let us not become weary in doing good, for at the proper time we will reap a harvest if we do not give up"* (Galatians 6:9 NIV). Wherever we are at the moment, we need to bloom where we are planted. Whatever the Lord is calling you to do, do the best because you may be called upon to assist in a season. While in that season, choose to be the best help possible. There may be a person the Lord wants you to reach. In the natural, you may not understand but ask the Lord for insight. He will always guide you and lead you.

Stay the Course

When we stay the course, we choose to follow and go with God's leading, God's flow. Staying the course allows you to see something to its completion. Distractions come to take you off the path; however, your job is to stay focused and do the things God is calling you to do. His plan for your life exceeds what you can see naturally. This is the time to stay in faith. Faith is what moves the hand of God. *"Faith shows the reality of what we hope for; it is the evidence of things we cannot see"* (Hebrews 11:1 NLT).

Focus

Some things are designed as distractions, and there are things aligned with your purpose. Do not allow the distractions to take you off course. No matter what, stay focused on your vision and what that looks like to you. Because everyone's vision is different, someone may have a dream to be a world-class athlete. At the same time, someone else may have the vision to be the best stay-at-home mom. Whatever your vision looks like to you, hold to that. Do not allow anyone to deter or diminish it. Keep pressing forward! As believers, we have to remember that the enemy's job is to distort or distract us from our God-given vision. *"I remain confident of this: I will see the goodness of the LORD in the land of the living"* (Psalm 27:13 NIV).

When we lack focus, it is because we are distracted and not paying attention to what we should do. Neville

Goddard once said, "You are only limited by weakness of attention and poverty of imagination!" Where your attention goes, your focus will also go there. And, when you are focused, your thoughts are directed towards what you want to create.

    One thing that helps me stay focused is trying to control my thoughts when I find myself getting distracted. I redirect them toward what I am working on and what I desire in my life. I turn them toward the vision I am working on, and I usually do this by speaking affirmations in my mind. I start speaking God's promises over my life. For example, if I am thinking about growing my business, I begin speaking affirmations about what I want to see (i.e., more clients, more paid gigs, speaking engagements, etc.) It is necessary to realize there are no limits to God. Whatever we desire to have, we can have it. Stay true and focused on your vision. Pastor Gregory Dickow said, "Our actions are a result of what we believe."

    A friend of mine had a goal to buy a house while selling the home she lived in. It seemed that it would be difficult in the natural, and people even told her that it may be impossible to sell one house while looking to buy another. In the natural, buying and selling a home entails a lengthy process, but she stayed focused on her vision. She told me she saw it in her mind before anything else because she held tight to what she wanted. To her, the vision was clear as day. She told me she saw it happening before it happened. This is the act of walking by faith. We move by what we see in our minds and do not allow outside circumstances to believe what we can and cannot accomplish.

Staying focused on what you want to create and accomplish is paramount to anything happening outside of you. Obstacles may come, but we should remain focused on what we believe and create as believers.

A Decided Mind

Once you make your mind up on something, try not to waver and stay rooted in what you decide. *"You can identify them by their fruit, that is, by the way they act..."* (Matthew 7:16 NLT). From what I have observed in today's culture, there are so many flip-flop things that seem to change every minute. When you look in the natural, there appears to be such instability in the way the world is. I believe it is because the world and its methods are not aligned with God's truth. You see, when things are rooted in reality, it does not change, especially God's truth. His Word says He is the same yesterday, today, and forever (Hebrews 13:8). Seasons may change, our lives may vary, but God's Word never changes. God is evident on how we are to conduct our lives. According to John 10:10, *The enemy comes to steal, kill, and destroy, but Jesus came so that we may have life more abundantly*. We should be rooted in the truth of God's Word and not the deception that is too often found in the world. A decided mind is a mind that is made up and knows clearly what it wants.

Scheduling Time

When we try to stay focused on our vision, we have to be intentional with our time. Distractions will come, but we have to decide not to let those distractions get in the way of what we want to accomplish. When I have a project that I am working on, I am intentional with my time. I may have to wake up earlier or rearrange my schedule to get it completed. One of the things I am learning is that it will not get done if I do not schedule a time to do it. I have to make proper use of my time. I have to be intentional with how I use the time God gave me. For example, a few months ago, the Lord put it on my heart that I need to incorporate exercise into my daily routine. Honestly, I am not that fond of exercising, but once I get started, I enjoy it. I realized if I do not make time for it. It will not happen.

Staying in God's Peace

As I said earlier, the world is ever-changing. One thing remains the same- God, His Word, His Character, and His Peace. The Word says, *"Then you will experience God's peace, which exceeds anything we can understand. His peace will guard your hearts and minds as you live in Christ Jesus"* (Philippians 4:7 NLT).

When you remain in God's peace, you are balanced. You are no longer moved to and fro by the things that are happening around you. It does not mean you will not experience an emotion towards something, but you will respond differently than how you responded before. You will look at the world through a different lens. Situations may arise, but you will be rooted in God's peace. The world may change, people may change, but God's peace and His Word will stay the same. I encourage you to reflect on and speak scriptures about God's peace over your life.

Earlier in the chapter, I spoke of a previous assignment. While there, another person talked to me and indicated that this might not be a temporary assignment and may be permanent. That brief exchange began to put a slight tinge of anxiety in me. When I felt the anxiousness creeping up, I immediately started to speak in my mind what I desired. Deep down inside, I knew I did not want to be there permanently. I was thankful for the opportunity, and I was grateful that God used me to serve. In my heart, I knew that was not where I wanted to be. I also understood that sometimes we might not fully understand why God does the things He does. It is important to allow God to guide you and bloom where you have been planted. In my mind, I decided while I was there, I would be the best help possible. I would serve and be the best team player possible. I encourage you wherever God has you today, choose to be your best, do the best, and serve wherever you can. Anything we go through, we grow through. God uses each and everything to get us to our appointed destination. The Word says *not to despise small beginnings* (Zechariah 4:10).

Self-First

We live in a world where putting yourself first may be deemed selfish while simultaneously putting yourself first is what is needed to "get ahead." As a believer, for the longest time, I had a hard time putting myself first. I thought that putting myself first was selfish, not Christian, and not showing God-like character. From speaking with other Christians, they have also felt the same way at times. It is almost like this belief that Christians are supposed to be meek all the time and doormats, we are not supposed to speak up for ourselves, and that we should give in all ways, even if we feel depleted. Yet, to be our best selves and the best version of who God created us to be, putting ourselves first is necessary. It is true; you cannot pour from an empty cup. The Word says to *"Love our neighbors as we love ourselves"* (Matthew 22:39). How can we genuinely love our neighbors if we do not love ourselves? This is why it is crucial to put yourself first. By this I mean, making sure you are stable in various ways, and then you will be a better help to someone else. Putting yourself first is not selfish. It is necessary to be beneficial to others.

    I want to share some practical, real-life examples. In the morning, before I begin my day, I may do several things. For example, spending time in prayer, reading His Word, speaking affirmations, going for a walk, etc. To me, these things are necessary for me to be my best self. I realize if I do not do these things, I am not my best self. There have been times, where I am in a rush in the morning and didn't spend time in prayer, and then I have an attitude and may get short with someone. This is why it is a necessity to put yourself first. Putting yourself first puts you in a better position to be of service to someone else. Your idea of putting yourself first may look different than mine.

Nonetheless, self-care is important. Many of us believers wear multiple hats, and we have numerous roles. In order to do them well, we need our self-first, self-care time. It is vital. I am a mother first. But I am also a daughter, sister, teacher, musician, minister, author, etc. Most of us have multiple things we are doing. So, it is essential to take time for yourself. When I was writing this book, I was writing amidst an unusual school year. I went back to in-person teaching during the 2020-2021 school year, and with all the challenges, I had to remain focused to do what I can efficiently. I also have a young son, and as a mom, I want him to be the best he can be and excel in every area of his life. It is important to have self-care because it adds balance to your life. With self-care, you learn not to overextend yourself. Years ago, I read the book "The Best Yes" by Lysa Terkeurst, and it talks about knowing when to say yes and when to say no. Sometimes, as Christians, we overextend ourselves. It's like we feel guilty for saying no. I know I used to feel bad about saying no to someone. Instead, I would say yes, and do the thing asked of me reluctantly. In some Christian circles, there is this belief that we are called to all things and all people. Jesus was not received everywhere (John 1:11). If Jesus was not received everywhere, what makes us think that we will be accepted everywhere? As believers, we have to continue to seek the Lord for direction and clarity on what we are called to do. This is why it is important to find balance in life. At times, I would say yes, knowing that my heart and mind were not into it. In my mind, I would not look bad or not look as though I was not living up to my Christian duty. Yet, the Word tells us," *When we do something, we should work as unto the Lord*" (Colossians 3:23). How can we work unto the Lord when our heart is not in it? This is why I have learned and continue to learn balance. When we do this, we can begin to live authentically. We commit to things that are aligned with our purpose with what God truly wants us to do.

Setting Boundaries

When we allow ourselves to be first and truly live authentically, we begin to realize what we will and will not tolerate. As I shared earlier, there is this belief that Christians are doormats. Even Jesus himself had boundaries. We sometimes forget that Jesus was both lion and lamb. Two examples from the Bible stand out for me. When Jesus needed time to rest and get away from the crowds, he did. In Luke 5:16, it says that Jesus often withdrew to pray and relax. We have to know when we should take time away. Doing this allows us to recharge, reset, and reorder to what God wants us to do. Having boundaries in place will enable us to protect our spirit.

Another example is when Jesus was upset with the vendors who were selling things in the temple. In Matthew 21:12, it says that he overturned the tables. He was very upset! In this scripture, Jesus was setting a boundary. He did not want commerce happening in his Father's house. We can learn a lot from Jesus because He was indeed about His Father's business. Jesus stayed the course and stayed focused on what He was called to do. He did not let anyone deter Him from His mission. We have to be the same way. Be so focused on your goals that anything not in alignment with it is a distraction.

As I told you before, I was put on an assignment. While on this assignment, I encountered a few people who clearly did not understand boundaries, or maybe I gave off the impression that my boundaries could be crossed. One day, as I was leaving the building, I was cornered by a person who two other people accompanied. She asked me a question that put me on the spot. I gave her a vague answer because, honestly, I thought what she asked me was unprofessional and unnecessary, especially in the presence of other people. It made me realize that people sometimes have the impression because I am a Christian and I am friendly, which means you may cross boundaries. People tend to think Christians are weak and docile. Not knowing that many Christians are full of discernment, have a prayer life, and understand dimensional living. This is why one of the principles I live by is "friendly with everybody, friends with few." We have to realize that everyone that appears friendly may not be your friend. I was appalled that she would ask such a thing, try to put me on the spot, and try to put another colleague down. In any environment that I am in, I try to operate to the best of my ability. *Do things with excellence and do it as unto the Lord* (Colossians 3:23). The good thing about this is, later on, she came to me and apologized because she realized it was out of order. This is another reason why I believe establishing boundaries is important. When we set boundaries, we teach people how to treat us. I understand no one is perfect. As believers, we are supposed to be operating in excellence with decency and order.

Feed Your Mind

"Every moment your mind is feeding on something on the subconscious level."- Reverend Ike…. Our mind is like a garden; what you plant in it is what will grow. So, I ask you today, what are you feeding your mind? Are you feeding it thoughts of success and abundance? Or are you feeding it thoughts of lack and despair? Each day we wake up, we have a choice. Either we will focus on what we want to create or focus on what is lacking in our lives. Whatever we feed our mind is what will manifest. I encourage you to choose wisely. *You will have what you say* (Mark 11:24). Daily we should choose to feed our minds on the things we want to create, not on the things showing up in the natural. I am intentional about the things I feed my mind.

Every day, I speak affirmations based on the things I want to create. The things I want to manifest and experience in my life are the things I focus on. I place my thoughts on continued health, building wealth, growing my business, continued health for family, success in all areas for Matthew. Your most repetitive and dominant thoughts are the ones that will manifest. I truly believe if we are not selective about what we feed our mind, the world will input in our minds what it will. To be honest, what the world feeds your mind is not good. We have to go deeper in our faith and feed our minds things that are beneficial to us in all areas of our lives. The only thing that matters is what you believe internally. Our thoughts create. Therefore, whatever we feed our mind is what will manifest. When you are clear on what you want, your focus will go in that direction, and you will feed your mind thoughts that align with what you want. When you are clear about what you want, you are clear about what will show up in your life.

We feed our mind through focusing on the right thoughts, speaking according to God's Will for our lives, and using our imagination to create the life we desire. Neville Goddard said, "Stop spending your time, your thoughts, and your money because everything in life must be an investment." When we feed our minds the right thoughts, we will put things beneficial to our lives. The Word says, "*We reap what we sow*"(Galatians 6:7). Whatever we sow into our mind will reap a harvest. Choose today what you will plant into your mind. Sow thoughts of success, favor, abundance, etc. Anything life-giving, feed that to your mind.

      I believe if we have a desire, it was given to us by God. Our desires are sacred. Meaning if you have the desire, it is intended for you. Do not allow outside circumstances, this 3D realm, to dictate what you will believe. We are so trained to focus only on what we see with our natural eyes. Our natural eyes are just a reflection of the things we see in this realm. We have to remember that our thoughts create. To create the life that we want, we have to look past the 3D realm. Often, when we focus on the 3D realm, it is negative. This is why the acronym for fear is, False Evidence Appearing Real. We have to step into who God intended for us to be. God is for you. You were created to live the life you deserve!

Our minds are like computers. Whatever programming we put in, we will experience it. I avoid watching negative things on purpose. For example, the news can incorporate so much negative programming on television, but most people do not realize it. When you begin to tune in to God's program, better known as His Word, you will begin to look at life through new lenses. Allow His Word to take root in your mind and saturate it so that you believe and speak in alignment with His Will for you. When we feed our minds the right things, we will produce the right results. We are all focusing on something, and we might as well focus on something that will bring positive changes to our lives. Everything in your outer world conforms to your beliefs. Your thoughts create your reality. This is why we have to be intentional about what we feed our minds. Suppose you have thoughts of lack, disappointment, failure, etc.; that is what you will experience. On the other hand, if you have thoughts of abundance, success, opportunities, etc., you will experience success. Every day we have the choice of what we will feed our mind. I encourage you to provide the right thoughts so that you will produce good fruit.

No Limits

We serve a mighty God! I am here to encourage you to let go of your limitations. The world is good at placing limitations on people. As carnal-minded people, we have been conditioned to believe that we want things we cannot have. That is absolutely not true. It is a limiting belief. If you have the desire and see it in your mind, you can experience it in your external world. I believe it is so important to know that we can live a limitless life. We serve an infinite God; therefore, there are no limits. I need you to believe that because the only limits are the ones we create. In earlier chapters of the book, we talked about the mind and thoughts. When we change our inner dialogue, our outer world will change. Speak as the limitless being you are. This is why I believe in speaking affirmations based on the Word of God. Our words have creative power. When we speak life-giving words, we give life to our reality. Our words have the power to shape and conform to the desired outcome. Repetition of affirmations is what creates reality. Anything you think upon consistently will solidify in your subconscious mind and then create. You will eventually experience the things your mind dwells on. Train yourself to focus only on the things you want and nothing else.

God can do above all that you ask, think, or imagine (Ephesians 3:20). Too often, we seek approval or validation from man on the very thing that God told us to do. When you fully step into who God created you to be and let go of limitations, life becomes less burdensome. You can have, be, and do whatever you want to do. When you let go of limitations, you let go of a limited mindset and anything that is not the true essence of who you were created to be. When you step into who God created you to be, you stop doubting yourself and needing other people's approval. You will soar like never before. You were given life so that you can experience what you want to on earth. It is incredible because when people cannot put you in a box or figure you out, they make assumptions that often are not true. If this happens, do not try to correct them.

Keep moving forward in the things God is calling you to do. Only God knows what He has placed inside of you.

Please understand when we live only by this finite realm, this realm of limitations, we do not truly tap into our potential. Always remember this natural realm is a realm of limitations while the supernatural realm is the faith realm, is the realm of possibilities. We serve a supernatural God! When God's super gets on your natural, there is nothing you cannot do. I believe when we live only by this dimension and allow other people's opinions to dictate what we believe, we end up second-guessing, doubting ourselves, and turning down what God has placed inside of us. This is the time to turn up and turn out on the things God has given you. Do not try to stay in a safe space. God is always calling us to higher dimensions in Him. I encourage you to step out into the things of God.

We are limitless when we know who we are. We are the expression of God in physical form. That is why the Word says we are *made in His image* (Genesis 1:27). We were put here on earth to experience life how we want to. Think the highest thoughts and dream the grandest dreams. I truly believe as we trust God and stay in faith, He will *give us the desires of our heart (*Psalm 37:4). As believers, we need to be more spirit-led. When we walk by faith and are led by the spirit, miracles, signs, and wonders become evident in our lives.

Activate Your Dream

All of us have been given dreams by God. I truly believe if you are still here, God has a plan and purpose for you. That plan and purpose for you exceed your current circumstances. Often, we have dreams, but we may feel that we cannot accomplish them. Some goals may seem so big that you are wondering in the natural how it will be done. Dreams are given to those who are willing to dream. A dream is something that will take you beyond where you are in the natural. Using our faith and the gift of imagination is so important. In your imagination, you can visualize and go anywhere you want. I encourage you not to allow your present circumstances to hinder your dreams. Life is happening in real-time. Many times, we wait until the conditions are optimal.

Newsflash…there will never be a "right" time to start the business, write the book, go back to school, or whatever your dreams are. Time waits for no one. Go after the vision that God has placed in your heart. *"I would have lost heart unless I had believed that I would see the goodness of the Lord in the land of the living"* (Psalm 27:13 NKJV). Whatever God has placed in your heart, go after it. Our dreams and desires are given to us by God. I want to leave this world empty, having used everything God gave me. If God places something on my heart that I want to accomplish. I make up in my mind that I am going to go after it. I will pursue it with everything in me. I realize I am relentless when I want something. I do not give up easily. I realize things may take time, but I believe if I see it in my mind, I will see it in the world.

It is so important to activate your dream. Zig Ziglar said, "You don't have to be great to start, but you have to start to be great." What do you want to accomplish before you leave this earth? Often, we think a dream may be something grand. Your vision may be to visit a country you have not toured before. I say go for it.

On the other hand, you may have a dream to start your own company. I say go for that too. You are never too old to fulfill the dream that God has placed on your heart. As I said earlier, we are God's expression on this earth. Honor the gifts and the dreams God gave you. You were born for such a time as this (Esther 4:14). The work you need to do is valuable. Someone needs what you have. When you accomplish your dreams, it will be a blessing to someone else. Our gifts are not for us. It is so that we can be a blessing to others. There is nothing we cannot do. I encourage you also to get around other dreamers. People who have dreams and a bigger vision for their life are visionaries. Get around other visionaries. They will help to fuel your dreams. They will encourage you when you want to give up and speak life into your imagination and help to fuel it. *"What you decide on will be done, and light will shine on your ways"* (Job 22:28 NIV). Believe in your dreams. Believe in your vision. More importantly, believe in God. We serve the God who created heaven and earth. *He has a great plan for you* (Jeremiah 29:11). Today, I encourage you to activate your dream.

Be Grateful

Sometimes, when we pursue a dream, we look at the time it takes to accomplish it. We may get so focused on the time that we forget to be grateful. Even a little bit of progress is still progress. One way to help us remain grateful is to remember that we have things we once prayed for. I think about how I once prayed for peace between my ex-husband and me because that situation at one point was tumultuous. At present, thanks to God and prayer, that situation is so peaceful now. It was something I once prayed for, and now it is here.

When we begin to look back and realize there are things that God has protected us from or blessed us with, we remain grateful. Having an attitude of gratitude is what brings forth blessings. You are responsible for your life. You are the only person who can give and assign meaning to the situations that occur in your life. Decide today how you will look at the conditions in your life. Are they good? Or are they wrong? The way you look at things is how things will show up in your reality. Create and envision your life on purpose. Affirm the things you want for your life and stick to them. Having a positive outlook towards life helps to keep your focus forward. Your attitude determines how you live your life. Will you live life being grateful or full of resentment? We have a choice as to how we will live our lives. I believe when we remain thankful, we allow God to do the miraculous in our lives.

One thing I will always remain grateful for is God's covering and protection. I look back on how God covered my family, friends, and coworkers during a pandemic year, and I am so grateful. As I listened to people who suffered tremendous loss, I realize God kept me. For that, I am eternally grateful. God is so good. He is so faithful!

Be Transformed

If we desire an abundant life, we must be transformed from the inside out. *"Do not conform to the pattern of this world but be transformed by the renewing of your mind. Then you will be able to test and approve what God's will is—his good, pleasing and perfect will"* (Romans 12:2 NIV). When we become transformed according to God's Will for our lives, the results are tremendous. In order for that to happen, we have to be open and receptive to what God wants to do in and through our lives. Change comes from within. It starts with our thoughts and beliefs. Our thoughts and beliefs need to come from the truth of God's Word. When this happens, we fully step into who God wants us to be. When we allow ourselves to be entirely changed to God's original intent, we become limitless.

How do we become transformed? We do this by allowing God's Word to take root in our lives. When we begin to shift our thinking and words, that is when a change will take place. I believe firmly in the power of prayer, speaking affirmations, and aligning our thoughts with what God says you can have, be, and do. Actor Sonny Franco said, "The best project you'll ever work on is you." When we become the best version of ourselves, there is nothing we cannot do. I encourage you today to begin to become transformed into who God is calling you to be.

Live Your Life

Once you realize that this is the one life God gave you, you will push forward with everything in you. We often make the mistake of being so focused on the past or the future that we forget to be present. Stay present in the moment. Stay consistent while waiting for God to answer that prayer and the manifestation in the now. Sometimes, we are waiting for the next best thing to be happy and live our life. Meanwhile, life is happening now. Look around you. What are some things you can be grateful for? I find it is in the everyday stuff that miracles still exist. God does His best work in us when we allow Him to lead us.

The Word says when we *acknowledge Him in all our ways, He will direct our paths* (Proverbs 3:6). I believe as we stay sensitive to the Holy Spirit working in our lives, we will see God's hand in everything. Learn to appreciate where you are now. Learn to accept and see what God is teaching you or walking you through. Take time for yourself. Be gentle with yourself as you transition into who God wants you to be. Discover new things. Learn a new skill. If there is something you enjoy doing, do it. If you like hiking, go on scenic hikes. If you enjoy exercising, start moving. Whatever God places on your heart to do, move in it. For myself, I love reading and writing near the water. Something about being by the water is so peaceful to me. I enjoy going out early in the morning to walk due to the stillness and quiet of nature during that time of day. My thoughts become more apparent when I walk. Sometimes I will pray or speak affirmations during that time. The Word says God *speaks in a still small voice* (1 Kings 19:11).

When we are attuned to God's voice, we will know what to do and how to proceed forward. We must stay in faith. Your faith and belief will move mountains. We have the power to change things around us through our views. *All things are possible for those that believe* (Mark 9:23). Know that everything that appears as a circumstance is working for you. God knows how to get us to our appointed destination. I encourage you to live life now. As we transform to God's way of thinking and live as the creators, we were designed to be, that is when you will see things change around you. Transformation starts within. I also want to encourage you that whatever you desire, believe that it is yours, and it will be.

Do not allow outside circumstances to dictate what you will and will not believe. Our thoughts create. As believers, we should learn to get our stability from God. Too often, we wait for external conditions to conform to what we want before we believe. Faith requires us to do the opposite. We must believe it first, then we will see it. And, yes, I understand, life may be overwhelming at times. Stabilize, align, and calm your thoughts to God's Word. My daily affirmations help keep me grounded and calm. The more we speak and believe according to God's Word, the more it will take root in our lives and begin to flourish. Begin to think about what you want. Speak affirmations aligned with what you are creating for your life. If you want to be wealthy, declare I am rich. If you want to be a successful business owner, say that now. We often wait on the outside circumstances to change before we declare who we are, not realizing that to change the circumstances, we must claim it now how we want it to be. I mentioned before that life is happening now and in real-time. God has wonderful things in store for you. To see it, you must believe. Believe in the best, the highest, grandest thing for your life, and it must show up. According to Job 22:28, "*What you decide on will be done.*" Decide to live your most extraordinary life today!

Affirmations

- I am focused
- I know how to create
- My life follows my thoughts
- I am guided by the truth of who God says I am
- I am successful
- I am discerning
- I always complete tasks easily and effortlessly
- I work efficiently
- I move with decisive action
- I am abundant
- I am flourishing
- I am wonderfully made by God
- I am open to receive divine downloads from God
- My mind is receptive to God's plan for me
- I am powerful
- I am created in God's image; therefore, I create
- I am attentive to my work
- I act and get things accomplished
- I work with enthusiasm and confidence
- I am committed to my goals

Journal Questions

1. In what ways will I eliminate distractions to enhance my life?

2. What affirmations will I speak daily to eliminate distractions?

Conclusion

When we choose to walk by faith and use the gift of imagination, the possibilities are endless. We are truly limitless when we tap into the power of God within us. As you use these tools, you will see that you will rise above the circumstances of life. When you truly begin to operate as a creator, the way God intended you to be, your life will start to elevate in numerous ways. *"God will always cause us to triumph"* (2 Corinthians 2:14). I encourage you to walk by faith daily and use the gift of imagination to create the life you desire. God wants you to live life and live it abundantly (John 10:10). Always look with the eyes of faith because faith opens the door for the miraculous to happen in your life. Remember to keep God first, and He will lead and guide you in your purpose. Remember, you were created to do remarkable things, be an overcomer!

Salvation Prayer

Father God, I believe that Jesus died for me so that I may have eternal life. I accept Him as my Lord and Savior. Please forgive me of my sins. Come into my heart and show me the right way to live. In Jesus' name, Amen!

Conclusion

When we choose to walk by faith and use the gift of imagination, the possibilities are endless. We are truly limitless when we tap into the power of God within us. As you use these tools, you will see that you will rise above the circumstances of life. When you truly begin to operate as a creator, the way God intended you to be, your life will start to elevate in numerous ways. *"God will always cause us to triumph"* (2 Corinthians 2:14). I encourage you to walk by faith daily and use the gift of imagination to create the life you desire. God wants you to live life and live it abundantly (John 10:10). Always look with the eyes of faith because faith opens the door for the miraculous to happen in your life. Remember to keep God first, and He will lead and guide you in your purpose. Remember, you were created to do remarkable things, be an overcomer!

Salvation Prayer

Father God, I believe that Jesus died for me so that I may have eternal life. I accept Him as my Lord and Savior. Please forgive me of my sins. Come into my heart and show me the right way to live. In Jesus' name, Amen!

Made in the USA
Las Vegas, NV
30 April 2024

89329136R00066